natural disasters

HURRICANES

Jil Fine

HIGH
interest
books

Children's Press
A Division of Scholastic Inc.
New York / Toronto / London / Auckland / Sydney
Mexico City / New Delhi / Hong Kong
Danbury, Connecticut

Book Design: Erica Clendening
Book Layout: Tahara Anderson
Contributing Editor: Jennifer Silate

Photo Credits: Cover © Roger Ressmeyer/Corbis; p. 4 © Marianne Todd/Getty Images; p. 6 Robyn Beck/AFP/Getty Images; p. 8 © Robert Sumner/Getty Images; p. 10 courtesy of the NOAA; p. 13 courtesy of the Image Science and Analysis Laboratory, NASA-Johnson Space Center; pp. 16, 28 © Mark Wilson/Getty Images; p. 19 courtesy of the US Army Corps of Engineers; p. 22 FEMA Photo/Mark Wolfe; pp. 24, 29 by NOAA via Getty Images; p. 27 © Chris Graythern/Getty Images; p. 30 by Jocelyn Augustino/FEMA; p. 32 © AP/Wide World Photos; p. 34 © Spencer Platt/Getty Images; pp. 35, 38 © Mario Tama/Getty Images; p. 36 by Michael Rieger/FEMA; p. 39 © Chip Somodevilla/Getty Images

Library of Congress Cataloging-in-Publication Data

Fine, Jil.
    Hurricanes / by Jil Fine.
    p. cm. - (Natural disasters)
    Includes index.
    ISBN-10: 0-531-12436-3 (lib. bdg.)   0-531-18722-5 (pbk.)
    ISBN-13: 978-0-531-12436-9 (lib. bdg.)   978-0-531-18722-7 (pbk.)
    1. Hurricanes-Juvenile literature. I. Title. II. Series.

    QC944.2.F56 2007
    363.34'922-dc22

                       2006006793

CONTENTS

The damage done by Hurricane Katrina to areas such as Biloxi, Mississippi, above, could take years to undo.

INTRODUCTION

On August 27, 2005, a state of emergency was declared for more than a million people living along the Gulf of Mexico. A hurricane named Katrina was moving rapidly across the gulf, threatening the people who lived on its coasts. Hurricane Katrina had already hit Florida. It had caused hundreds of millions of dollars of damage and killed several people there.

Forecasters warned the people living in Louisiana, Mississippi, and Alabama that the powerful hurricane was on its way. More than a million people were told to leave their homes.

On Monday, August 29, 2005, Hurricane Katrina made landfall. For several hours, Katrina pounded the Gulf Coast with winds of more than 100 miles (160 kilometers) per hour. The hurricane caused water from the Gulf of Mexico to flood inland. The cities of Biloxi and Gulfport in Mississippi, were almost completely destroyed by winds and flooding. The rising

In this photo, cars travel on a highway flooded by Hurricane Katrina in Cameron Parish, along the Gulf Coast of Louisiana.

waters flooded levees—strong walls to keep the city dry—in New Orleans, Louisiana. This sent millions of tons of water into the city streets.

By 11:00 A.M. the next morning, Katrina had calmed down a little. The damage that it caused in just a few hours, however, was more than anyone could have imagined. New Orleans was no longer a safe place for people to live. The floodwaters brought in sewage, toxic waste, and other pollutants. There was no electricity or running water. Thousands of people were trapped by the floodwaters. Homes and businesses were destroyed. People's lives were changed overnight by the devastation. Hurricane Katrina killed more than 1,300 people. It caused billions of dollars worth of damage.

For decades, scientists have worked to understand what causes these powerful storms and to try to predict what path they will take. Read on to learn more about these natural disasters and what you can do if you ever find yourself in a hurricane's path.

Thick, gathering clouds can be a signal that heavy winds and rainfall are approaching an area.

chapter 1

THE BIRTH OF A HURRICANE

T he word "hurricane" comes from Hurican—the name of the Caribbean god of evil. A hurricane is a large and powerful storm. Some hurricanes can stretch for over 600 miles (966 km). A hurricane may only move 10 or 20 miles (16 or 32 km) per hour across the ocean. The strongest winds of a hurricane, however, can reach up to 200 miles (320 km) per hour.

THE BEGINNING

A hurricane starts as a group of thunderstorms in the Atlantic basin (an area that includes the Atlantic Ocean, the Caribbean Sea, and the Gulf of Mexico). Most hurricanes form off Africa's west coast. Winds from the Northern and Southern Hemispheres come together there. This air heats up over the warm ocean water. The warm air rises and carries moisture up into the sky. As the air cools, clouds are created. Back down on the surface of the ocean,

HOW A HURRICANE FORMS

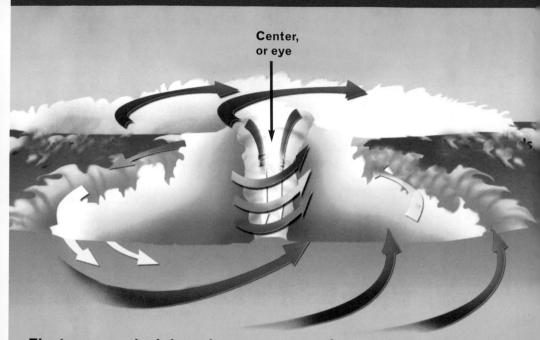

Center, or eye

First, warm air rising above an ocean forms clouds. As more air rises, more clouds are made. Earth's rotation causes the clouds to spin, creating the swirling effect of a hurricane. The center of the hurricane is called the eye.

cool air is forced into the area left by the heated air. This air is also heated and rises. As more air is forced up, more clouds are made. Eventually, Earth's movement as it rotates on its axis makes the giant towers of clouds spin around the area where the warm air rises.

FIRST, A TROPICAL DEPRESSION

When a hurricane is just beginning, the movement of warm, moist air creates strong thunderstorms. If the water is 80 degrees Fahrenheit (27 degrees Celsius) or warmer, enough air can be heated to continue to strengthen the thunderstorms. The rains get heavier and the winds get faster. As this group of thunderstorms grows in strength, it becomes a tropical depression. Tropical depressions have winds that maintain a speed of up to 38 miles (56 km) per hour. If a tropical depression continues to move across warm waters and is not broken up by strong winds from another direction, then it may grow into a tropical storm.

DID YOU KNOW?

Due to Earth's rotation, hurricanes spin in different directions above and below the equator. Above the equator, hurricanes spin counter-clockwise. Below the equator, they spin clockwise. The same thing happens when water goes down the drain of your sink!

THE TROPICAL STORM

A tropical storm has winds that maintain speeds between 39 and 73 miles (63 and 118 km) per hour. On average, ten tropical storms develop each year in the Atlantic basin. Scientists give tropical storms names. Naming storms helps scientists keep track of individual storms more easily. A tropical storm becomes a hurricane when it builds even more energy and its winds

WHEN IS A HURRICANE NOT A HURRICANE?

Any tropical storm with winds that move more than 73 miles (118 km) per hour is called a tropical cyclone. If it forms in the Atlantic basin, we call it a hurricane. In the western Pacific Ocean, it is known as a typhoon. In the Indian Ocean, such a storm is called a cyclone. These powerful storms will strike at different times of the year throughout the world.

increase to 74 miles (119 km) per hour. A hurricane keeps the name it was given as a tropical storm.

THE PARTS OF THE STORM: THE EYE

Once a hurricane forms, it has three parts: the eye, the eye wall, and rain bands. The eye is

This photo of a developing tropical storm was taken from the International Space Station, orbiting high above Earth.

the center of the hurricane. The eye has very low air pressure. Air pressure is the weight of air molecules in the atmosphere. Since air is a gas, molecules can blow around and are not spread out evenly. Low pressure is when there are few air molecules clumped together. Warm air quickly rises in the eye and leaves behind an area of low pressure near the surface of the ocean.

The skies in the eye of a hurricane are calm and have very few clouds. A hurricane's eye can be between 20 and 30 miles (32 and 48 km) wide. The calm weather in the eye of a hurricane can trick people into believing that the storm is over when they are really just in the center of it.

THE EYE WALL

The eye wall is a column of clouds around the eye of a hurricane. The eye wall is where the most powerful winds and rains are in the hurricane. Air moves quickly toward the eye of the hurricane, but cannot enter it. Instead of entering the eye, the air is suddenly pushed up as if it had hit a wall. This produces violent winds and rain. The eye wall of Hurricane Katrina was 30 miles (48 km) wide when it hit land.

RAIN BANDS

The storm clouds of a hurricane form spiral bands around the eye. These bands are called rain bands. Rain bands spread for hundreds of miles. Most of the areas affected by hurricanes have been hit only by the hurricane's rain bands. Even though the rain bands are not as violent as the eyewall, they can still have enough power to do a lot of damage.

'TIS THE SEASON

Conditions must be just right for a hurricane to form. The water must be 80 degrees Fahrenheit (27 degrees C) or warmer in order to heat the air above and give it moisture. The winds must also continually blow in one direction to keep the air moving up from the surface of the ocean.

There are usually only certain months of the year when conditions are right for hurricanes to form. In the Atlantic Ocean, that time is from June 1 to November 30. This time of year is called hurricane season.

Hurricane Katrina's high winds and heavy rain whipped through the streets of New Orleans, leaving destruction in its wake.

chapter 2

UNDERSTANDING HURRICANES

Hurricanes have caused billions of dollars worth of damage and killed thousands of people. Their powerful winds and rains can destroy buildings, flood cities, and send cars flying through the air.

WIND POWER

High winds are a major threat to people and property during a hurricane. A hurricane loses power as it leaves warm water and moves over land. Its winds, however, can still remain at hurricane force for many miles inland. Winds can pick up trees, street signs, and even cars.

TWISTERS

A hurricane's winds can also produce tornadoes. Tornadoes are smaller, spinning storms that are very intense. They have winds of 250 miles (402 km) per hour or greater. The tornadoes formed during a hurricane are not the strongest tornadoes possible. But together with the winds of a hurricane they can be very dangerous. Most tornadoes occur to the right and in front of the eye of a hurricane. This is where the strongest winds of a hurricane are located.

STORM SURGE

In addition to the destructive power of high winds on land, very strong winds also blow water onto the shore. This is called a storm surge. A storm surge causes the water levels to rise. Storm surges are often accompanied by rough waves that are also created by the violent winds. These waves can pound millions of tons of water against buildings, causing many to collapse. A storm surge that happens when the tide is already high can cause devastating results. The storm surge during Katrina rose about 20 feet (6 meters) and was a major reason the levees failed.

FLOODING

Most of the people who die during a hurricane do so as a result of inland flooding. The heavy rainfall of a hurricane can quickly result in widespread flooding. Streams, rivers, and storm drains flood in heavy rain. When this happens,

Storm surges can create high, powerful waves that are capable of causing massive destruction.

the excess water spills over onto dry land. Swiftly moving floodwaters can sweep away people and even cars.

MEASURING THE STORM

Scientists have created a scale that rates hurricanes from one to five, with five being the most powerful. This scale is called the Saffir-Simpson hurricane scale. It is used to let people know just how strong a hurricane is and what precautions they should take if it is approaching where they live.

STUDYING THE STORMS: SATELLITES

Scientists use many different technologies to study hurricanes. Governments send satellites into space to take pictures of Earth. Satellites can send these pictures to scientists on the ground. Scientists use these pictures to study the size, shape, and path of developing storms. Right now, U.S. satellites above Earth take pictures of the entire Atlantic Ocean every half an hour.

RADAR

Doppler radar is also used by scientists to track weather. A Doppler radar transmitter sends out radio waves from weather stations. The waves hit an object, such as a building or raindrop, and scatter in all directions. Some of those waves return to the radar dish. Those waves are then analyzed to find how long it took for the waves to hit the object and get back to the station.

THE SAFFIR-SIMPSON HURRICANE SCALE

- **Category One:** Winds are 74 to 95 miles (119 to 153 km) per hour. Coastal flooding may occur.
- **Category Two:** Winds are 96 to 110 miles (154 to 177 km) per hour. Trees, roofs, and windows can be damaged.
- **Category Three:** Winds are 111 to 130 miles (179 to 209 km) per hour.
- **Category Four:** Winds are 131 to 155 miles (211 to 249 km) per hour. The force of these winds can severely damage houses and knock over trees.
- **Category Five:** Winds are 156 miles (251 km) per hour or greater. Buildings will be heavily damaged. Katrina was a Category Five storm.

Instruments then use these measurements to figure out how much rain is falling, how fast the wind is moving, and where the eye, eye wall, and rain bands are in a hurricane.

HURRICANE HUNTERS

Some scientists like to study hurricanes up close. They use specially designed airplanes to

Federal Emergency Management Association (FEMA) workers track the progress of a hurricane.

fly into hurricanes and make their observations. They are called hurricane hunters. They measure wind speed, wind direction, air pressure, and temperature, among other things. They drop small radio devices called dropsondes into the hurricane. These objects take measurements as they fall. Dropsondes record measurements twice each second!

Scientists use these technologies to watch developing storms and help keep track of hurricanes. As technology improves, so does scientists' ability to predict when and where a hurricane will strike.

This satellite image of Hurricane Katrina shows the storm as it works its way through the Gulf of Mexico.

chapter 3

THE PATH OF DESTRUCTION

On August 23, 2005, a group of thunderstorms near the Bahamas formed the tropical depression that would become Katrina. The depression strengthened into a hurricane over the next two days. On August 25, Katrina hit Florida. It was then a Category One hurricane on the Saffir-Simpson scale. The strong winds and rains blasted Florida, killing fourteen people. Unfortunately, this was only a hint of what was to come.

GROWING IN THE GULF

Over the next few days, Katrina strengthened rapidly. After hitting Florida, it traveled hundreds of miles over the warm waters of the Gulf of Mexico. Katrina grew so large that its clouds covered almost the entire gulf. That is an area about the size of Alaska! By August 28, 2005, Katrina was a Category Five hurricane. Its winds were moving at 175 miles (280 km) per hour.

DID YOU KNOW?

The year 2005 was a record-breaking year for tropical storms. There were twenty-seven named storms in 2005, the most ever in one year. Eight of those storms, including four major hurricanes, hit the United States.

The people living along the Gulf Coast were warned that the powerful hurricane was quickly coming their way.

A CITY IN TROUBLE

New Orleans is built on land that sits 6 feet (1.8 m) below sea level. Levees keep the city dry during normal weather. Scientists feared that the damaging winds and storm surge might damage the levees and flood the city.

Government officials told the more than 460,000 residents of New Orleans to leave the city. People crowded the highways in an attempt to flee the hurricane. Some people, however, had to stay behind. Many people who were elderly, sick, or poor could not leave. There was no plan in place to get those who did not have a car or

Once warned of Hurricane Katrina's approach, many New Orleans residents took to the roads to escape the destruction that was headed their way.

enough money to leave the city out in time. As
the hurricane approached, thousands of people
who were still inside New Orleans went to the
Superdome football stadium for shelter. The rest
would ride out the storm at home or elsewhere
in the city. All along the coast, people prepared

**Even the Superdome wasn't safe from the waist-deep
floodwaters of Katrina.**

for what experts were forecasting to be one of the worst storms to ever hit the area.

KATRINA ATTACKS

Hurricane Katrina hit Louisiana around 6:00 A.M. on August 29. Its winds had slowed to those of a Category Three storm. However, because of its size and the strength it had built up while in the gulf, Katrina was much more devastating

In Washington, D.C., National Guardsmen prepare their gear before being sent to the Gulf Coast to aid the victims of Katrina.

than most Category Three hurricanes. Winds were damaging at 125 miles (201 km) per hour and gusting much higher. The winds knocked limbs off trees, tore down power lines, and ripped apart homes. Even parts of the roof of the Superdome, where thousands had gone for safety, were torn off by the winds.

The storm surge rose greatly along the coast. Flooding was reported in Louisiana, Mississippi,

Levee

This photo shows floodwaters as they surge over a levee in **New Orleans.**

and Alabama. Homes, businesses, boats, and even entire towns were destroyed. In some are floodwaters reached 12 miles (19 km) inland.

By the end of the day, several of New Orleans' levees had failed. Water poured in. In some places, water rose to 20 feet (6.1 m) deep. People still in their homes fled to their attics or rooftops to escape the rising waters. About 80 percent of New Orleans was flooded.

AFTER THE STORM

By the next morning, the storm had greatly weakened. Winds that had once been blowing upward of 175 miles (282 km) per hour at the hurricane's peak had decreased to 35 miles (56 km) per hour. The worst of the hurricane was over, but the people left in New Orleans were still not safe. For many of them, getting food, water, and shelter would be another problem they had to face.

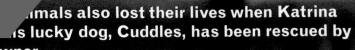

...mals also lost their lives when Katrina ...s lucky dog, Cuddles, has been rescued by ...owner.

chapter 4

PICKING UP THE PIECES

I n the hours after Katrina struck, reports from New Orleans told of the enormous amount of damage there. Many people were without food, water, or medical care.

Most roads into the areas affected were too dangerous to travel during the storm because of high winds and flooding. Many emergency response teams from the Federal Emergency Management Agency (FEMA) were not able to help those in need until the day after the storm hit. People were stuck on their rooftops, surrounded by floodwaters. Sewage, oil, and toxic waste had spilled into those waters.

THE WAIT

Medical supplies were low. Some hospitals had to be shut down after the hurricane due to flooding or lack of electricity. Some people died because they did not get the medical attention they needed immediately after the storm. Neither

People called **FEMA** from emergency phone centers to get water, food, electricity, and other supplies.

the city nor the nation had been prepared for a disaster as big as Katrina.

In the days after Katrina, temperatures soared to 100 degrees Fahrenheit (38 degrees C). Though the Superdome had been used as a shelter, city officials had not been able to get

DID YOU KNOW?

The military response to Katrina was the largest ever in the United States for a natural disaster.

enough food and water there for everyone. Some people left in the city stole from grocery stores to get the food and water they desperately needed.

The first attempts to repair the levees failed. The waters continued to rise in some areas. The mayor of the city announced that everyone who was left in the city must leave. It was not safe for people to live there. Helicopters and boats were brought in to take everyone out of New Orleans.

Many residents of New Orleans were flown to shelters in other states because their homes had been destroyed.

REPAIRING AND REBUILDING

Experts think the total cost of Katrina may top $200 billion. It was the most expensive hurricane in history. In addition to all of the homes and buildings that were destroyed, many other things were damaged by the hurricane. Sewer, water, electricity, and gas

The clean up begins as two homeowners work to repair their house following the destruction left by Katrina.

36

systems needed to be fixed. The water that had flooded the city of New Orleans had to be pumped out and the levees had to be repaired.

Out in the gulf, several oil rigs were damaged or destroyed. The damage caused the price of oil to surge throughout the country. It also spilled millions of gallons of oil into the polluted waters of Louisiana and Mississippi. The future effects of this pollution on the environment and the health of the people who live nearby are still unknown.

COMING BACK HOME

Over the next few months, life along the Gulf Coast slowly started to return to normal. People repaired and rebuilt their homes where they could. Three months after the hurricane, about half of New Orleans had electricity and gas service again. One public school and about 1,100 businesses reopened. Only one-quarter of the residents of New Orleans were able to return. People continue to work hard to get the city reopened and its citizens safely back home and working—a process that could take several years.

FIXING MISTAKES

The federal and state governments are also working to make sure they will be better prepared if another hurricane or major natural disaster strikes the United States. The federal government has changed its emergency response plans so that help and supplies will be sent before a storm hits. Emergency workers will

IN THE PATH OF A HURRICANE

What should you do if you find yourself in a hurricane's path? Here are some tips:

• Make a plan as a family; know where you will go in the event of a hurricane.

• Create a disaster emergency kit. Include batteries, a flashlight, a battery-operated radio, canned food, water, blankets, and first-aid supplies.

• Secure your home and property. High winds can move outdoor furniture, flowerpots, and many other things.

Protestors in front of the White House voice their anger over the federal government's poor handling of the Gulf Coast disaster.

also have their own networks of communications that are not dependent on cell phone towers or telephone lines. State governments across the country are also developing plans to help their citizens should a disaster happen where they live.

Hurricane Katrina took more than 1,300 lives. Some of those people might have been saved if the state and federal governments had been better prepared. Officials are working hard to make sure that the next time a natural disaster strikes, they'll be ready.

North
America

Atlantic Ocean

Gulf of
Mexico

Caribbean
Sea

South
America

HISTORY'S EIGHT DEADLIEST
HURRICANES

1 Great Hurricane of 1780 (Lesser Antilles)
1780 **22,000** deaths

2 Hurricane Mitch (Honduras/Central America)
1998 **11,000–18,000** deaths

3 Galveston Hurricane of 1900 (Texas)
1900 **6,000–12,000 deaths**

4 Hurricane Fifi (Belize)
1974 **8,000–10,000 deaths**

5 1930 Dominican Republic Hurricane
1930 **2,000–8,000 deaths**

6 Hurricane Flora (Haiti and Cuba)
1963 **7,200–8,000 deaths**

7 Newfoundland Hurricane
1775 **4,000 deaths**

8 Okeechobee Hurricane (Bahamas/Florida)
1928 **4,000 deaths**

Africa

NEW WORDS

Doppler radar (**dah**-pluhr **ray**-dar) a system that sends out continuous radio waves to measure the speed and direction of storms

dropsonde (**drop**-sond) an instrument dropped from an aircraft that measures temperature, humidity, pressure, and winds

equator (i-**kway**-tur) an imaginary line around the middle of Earth, halfway between the north and south poles

eye (**eye**) the calm, clear zone at the very center of a hurricane

eye wall (**eye wahl**) a column of clouds around the eye of a hurricane; the most violent storms are in the eye wall

hurricane (**hur**-uh-kane) a violent storm with high winds that starts in the areas of the Atlantic basin near the equator and then travels north, northeast, or northwest

hurricane hunters (**hur**-uh-kane **huhnt**-urz) scientists who fly into hurricanes to study them

hurricane season (**hur**-uh-kane **see**-zuhn) the time of year when hurricanes are most active, from June 1 to November 30

levees (**lev**-eez) banks or walls built up near a river to prevent flooding

NEW WORDS

rain bands (**rayn bandz**) the bands of clouds that spiral outward from the eye of a hurricane

Saffir-Simpson scale (**saf**-fer **simp**-son **skale**) a way of defining the strength of a hurricane, from one to five

satellites (**sat**-uh-lites) spacecraft that are sent into orbit around Earth or other heavenly bodies, often to take pictures of weather patterns and send them to scientists for study

storm surge (**storm surj**) a rise in water level on shore created by hurricane force winds over open water

tornadoes (tor-**nay**-dohz) swirling columns of air that appear as a dark cloud shaped like a funnel

tropical cyclone (**trop**-uh-kuhl **sye**-klone) a storm over warm waters with very strong, destructive winds that blow around a quiet center; hurricanes, typhoons, and cyclones are all tropical cyclones

tropical depression (**trop**-uh-kuhl di-**presh**-uhn) a storm over warm waters with winds up to 38 miles (61 km) per hour

tropical storm (**trop**-uh-kuhl **storm**) a storm over warm waters with winds from 39 to 73 miles (62 to 117 km) per hour

FOR FURTHER READING

Ceban, Bonnie. *Hurricanes, Typhoons, and Cyclones: Disaster and Survival.* Berkeley Heights, NJ: Enslow Publishers, 2005.

Demarest, Chris L. *Hurricane Hunters!: Riders on the Storm.* New York: Margaret K. McElderry, 2006.

Gaffney, Timothy R. *Hurricane Hunters.* Berkeley Heights, NJ: Enslow Publishers, 2001.

Lauber, Patricia. *Hurricanes: Earth's Mightiest Storms.* New York: Scholastic, 1996.

Spilsbury, Louise. *Howling Hurricanes.* Portsmouth, NH: Heinemann, 2004.

RESOURCES

ORGANIZATIONS

Federal Emergency Management Agency

500 C Street, SW

Washington, D.C. 20472

Phone: (202) 566-1600

http://www.fema.gov

The National Hurricane Center

11691 SW 17th Street

Miami, FL 33165

http://www.nhc.noaa.gov

World Meteorological Organization

7 bis, avenue de la Paix

Casè Postale No. 2300

CH-1211 Geneva 2

Switzerland

E-mail: wmo@wmo.int

http://www.wmo.int

RESOURCES

WEB SITES

FEMA for Kids: Hurricanes
www.fema.gov/kids/hurr.htm
This Web site has a lot of information about
hurricanes, including pictures, true stories,
interesting facts, and tips on how to stay safe
if a hurricane threatens where you live.

Hurricanes: National Geographic for Kids
www.nationalgeographic.com/ngkids/0308/
hurricane/
Learn about hurricanes, hurricane hunters, and
survival tips on this Web site.

Tropical Twisters
kids.earth.nasa.gov/archive/hurricane
Find out more about hurricanes and complete
a word search on this site.

INDEX

INDEX

ABOUT THE AUTHOR

Jil Fine has written more than one hundred titles for children. She is a member of the Society of Children's Book Writers and Illustrators.